Uncharted, Unexplored, and Unexplained

Scientific Advancements of the 19th Century

Alexander Graham Bell

and the Story of the Telephone

Mitchell Lane
PUBLISHERS

P.O. Box 196
Hockessin, Delaware 19707

Uncharted, Unexplored, and Unexplained

Scientific Advancements of the 19th Century

Titles in the Series

Visit us on the web: www.mitchelllane.com
Comments? email us: mitchelllane@mitchelllane.com

Scientific Advancements of the 19th Century

Alexander Graham Bell

and the
Story of the Telephone

by John Bankston

Uncharted, Unexplored, and Unexplained

Scientific Advancements of the 19th Century

Copyright © 2005 by Mitchell Lane Publishers, Inc. All rights reserved. No part of this book may be reproduced without written permission from the publisher. Printed and bound in the United States of America.

Printing   1   2   3   4   5   6   7   8

Library of Congress Cataloging-in-Publication Data
Bankston, John, 1974-
    Alexander Graham Bell and the story of the telephone / John Bankston.
        p. cm. — (Uncharted, unexplored & unexplained)
    Includes bibliographical references and index.
    Contents: An important lesson — Parts of speech — Varied lessons — Phoning Watson — Always the inventor.
    ISBN 1-58415-243-5 (Library Bound)
1. Bell, Alexander Graham, 1847-1922—Juvenile literature. 2. Inventors—United States—Biography—Juvenile literature. 3. Telephone—United States—History—Juvenile literature. [1. Bell, Alexander Graham, 1847-1922. 2. Inventors. 3. Telephone—History.] I. Title. II. Series.
    TK6143.B4B36 2004
    621.385'092--dc22
                                                        2003024046

ABOUT THE AUTHOR: Born in Boston, Massachussetts, **John Bankston** began publishing articles in newspapers and magazines while still a teenager. Since then, he has written over two hundred articles, and contributed chapters to books such as *Crimes of Passion*, and *Death Row 2000*, which have been sold in bookstores across the world. He has written numerous biographies for young adults, including *Joseph Lister and the Story of Antiseptics* and *Louis Daguerre and the Story of the Daguerreotype* (Mitchell Lane). He currently lives in Portland, Oregon.

PHOTO CREDITS: Cover: SuperStock; p. 6 Hulton|Archive; p. 9 Hulton|Archive; p. 12 Hulton|Archive; p. 17 Hulton|Archive; p. 18 Hulton|Archive; p. 22 Hulton|Archive; p. 24 Hulton|Archive; p. 27 Corbis; p. 30 Science Photo Library; p. 36 Hulton|Archive; p. 38 Science Photo Library

PUBLISHER'S NOTE: This story is based on the author's extensive research, which he believes to be accurate. Documentation of such research is contained on page 47.

The internet sites referenced herein were active as of the publication date. Due to the fleeting nature of some web sites, we cannot guarantee they will all be active when you are reading this book.

Uncharted, Unexplored, and Unexplained

Scientific Advancements of the 19th Century

Alexander Graham Bell

and the Story of the Telephone

*For Your Information

This photograph shows a woman in the 1960s teaching a deaf child. Alexander Graham Bell and his father, Alexander Melville Bell, gave speech lessons and taught deaf children with Melville's invention of the "Visible Speech System."

1

An Important Lesson

Five-year-old George Sanders bounded into his playroom and begged for a toy from his teacher. Because the little boy had been deaf since birth, he didn't speak or yell. Instead, he had his own private sign for what he wanted. He folded his arms and struck his shoulders with his hands. But instead of giving George his toy, his teacher just looked confused.

This was unexpected. Whenever George had made this sign before, his teacher would give him what he was "asking" for. This time it didn't work.

It was 1872. The two were in George's grandmother's house in Salem, Massachusetts. His teacher rented a room upstairs. For the last few weeks, he'd been changing the game.

Young George would signal for his doll.

"The doll was accordingly produced," as his teacher noted later. "His (George's) attention was directed to the word 'doll' pasted upon the forehead. We compared this word with the words written upon the cards, to see who would first find the card with the word 'doll' upon it."[1]

Without even knowing it, George was learning how to read. So on this particular day, his teacher pretended not to understand the boy's very personal sign.

"I produced a toy horse; but that was not what he wanted," the teacher continued. "A table; still he was disappointed. He seemed quite perplexed to know what to do, and evidently considered me very stupid. At last, in desperation, he went to the card-rack and, after a moment's consideration, pulled out the word 'doll' and presented it to me. It is needless to say that the coveted toy was at once placed into his possession."[2]

The teacher wasn't just teaching George how to read. He was teaching him how to communicate.

Being able to communicate is a basic need of all living things. Some of the smallest organisms rely on chemical signals. Social insects such as ants and bees have elaborate methods of giving directions to food supplies. Ancient humans perfected both sound and smoke signals that allowed them to "speak" even when they were separated by long distances.

During the early days of the United States, some messages were relayed by semaphore. Standing on top of a tall hill and using a pair of colored flags, signalers would indicate a single letter of the alphabet depending upon how the flags were held. In that manner, messages could slowly be relayed down a long line of signalers. By the late 1700s, the government of the new United States had offered a $30,000 prize to anyone who could design a similar system that would extend along the entire Atlantic Coast. The prize description gave that proposed system a name: telegraph.

In 1844, Samuel Morse used electricity, not flags, for his telegraph. With this new technology, people soon gained the ability to communicate effectively over hundreds, even thousands, of miles. The world seemed a little bit smaller. For example, someone in Boston, Massachusetts could send a message to a business partner in the Midwest, on the Pacific Coast or even overseas.

Telegraph machines, pictured here, were the first devices to send messages by electricity. To send messages over the telegraph, the letters of the alphabet were converted into a dot-dash code developed by Samuel Morse. The telegraph changed the Morse code into electrical signals and sent them over telegraph wires.

The telegraph was a great achievement, but it was loaded with drawbacks. For one thing, the best forms of communication are two-way streets. People have a back-and-forth conversation, with questions and immediate answers. But when a telegraph message was sent, it had to be decoded and written out. Then the recipient had to send back a reply. In modern terms, it was similar to sending an e-mail rather than using instant messaging.

The whole process took a long time. Since signal strength varied, messages often took over a day to reach their destination. It was so expensive that few private individuals could afford it, except for special occasions. As a result, it was mainly a business tool. Using a telegraph also required specialized training.

It took George Sanders' teacher—a teacher of the deaf—to figure out a better way for people to speak to each other over long distances. The son and grandson of celebrated speakers, he was the child of a deaf mother. He began his experiments hoping to improve on the human voice box and offer deaf people a better way to communicate. By the time he developed the telephone, he was motivated partly by love and partly by money. He'd fallen in *love* with one of his students and he needed *money* to prove to her father that he could support her if he married her. A successful invention could provide that money.

He didn't just devise a new form of the telegraph. Instead, he invented an entirely new device, one that could be used by anyone.

"The great advantage it possesses over every other form of electrical apparatus consists in the fact that it requires no skill to operate the instrument,"[3] he later wrote in a letter.

This instrument would change the way that people communicate around the world. It is the telephone, and its inventor's name is Alexander Graham Bell.

In 1832, an American artist named Samuel Morse was on a ship coming back from a European trip, and he felt out of touch. Once they left land, ships were unable to communicate with shore. Often they sank without warning, leaving bewildered greeters waiting on docks and wondering what had happened.

Samuel Morse

Morse wondered about the possibility of using electricity to communicate across vast distances. He'd been fascinated by lectures about the power of electricity while he was a student at Yale, but he had little understanding of how it worked. Once his ship reached land, Morse set out to discover all he could. With the aid of Leonard Gale, a fellow professor at the University of the City of New York, he spent the next five years trying to develop a way of sending messages over a wire. By 1837, Morse was able to demonstrate a crude telegraph.

His timing could not have been worse. The country was in the midst of a severe economic downturn. Neither the government nor private individuals had money to spare for Morse's invention. It wasn't until 1843 that he was finally able to convince the government to fund a telegraph line from Baltimore, Maryland to Washington, D.C., a distance of about forty miles. The following year he sent the first-ever telegraph message. It was "What hath God wrought?"

Morse's telegraph was a fairly simple device. At one end of the line, an operator would slide a pointer connected to a battery and a wire across long and short bars. The bars produced patterns of dashes and dots, each of which corresponded to a letter in the alphabet or a number. On the other side of the line an operator would "decode" the message and write it down.

Although it would still be some time before ships could communicate with shore, the steamship Great Eastern laid the first transatlantic telegraph cable in 1866. Europe and North America were now "wired" and could communicate through Morse's telegraph.

This photograph of Alexander Graham Bell was taken in 1905. Bell is the man credited with inventing the telephone, though many others have tried to take credit for it. Bell fought over 600 lawsuits in his lifetime to protect his invention.

2

Parts of Speech

The mill owner looked at eleven-year-old Aleck, the name by which everyone called young Alexander, and asked him a question he'd never forget: "Why don't you do something useful?"[1] The boy was a bit of a troublemaker, but he already had demonstrated two qualities vital to every successful inventor. He was curious and he was persistent. There was nothing unusual about that. Having a sense of wonder and refusing to give up ran in the family.

Aleck was named after his grandfather, who'd been a shoemaker in Scotland in the early 1800s. There was nothing wrong with making shoes. The job was respectable and paid a decent wage. It just wasn't enough for the senior Alexander. He left the family trade for acting, a profession with little respect and poor pay. He appeared in numerous stage productions before deciding to do more. He turned to public speaking, and earned a reputation more for his voice than for his opinions. His work on stage had trained him to hide his thick Scottish brogue. Soon after he began his speaking engagements, wealthy audience members began hiring him to give speech lessons. Upper-class Englishmen paid well for their instruction from the former Scottish shoemaker. Alexander earned a fine living and began a new family tradition.

His son, Alexander Melville Bell (called Melville by family and friends alike) also gave speech lessons. He taught at the University of Edinburgh and offered private tutorials to reduce stuttering, lisping and accents. In his free time he wrote speech textbooks and created a new alphabet. His "Visible Speech System" was a phonetic alphabet, in which each symbol represented a specific sound. For example, an English speaker who used the system could easily pronounce French words. When he completed it in 1864, Melville would become even more successful than his father.

Understanding speech was vital in the Bell household. Melville's wife, Eliza, was almost completely deaf. Using an ear tube, an unwieldy device held up to the ear, Eliza could sometimes make out the voices of her family. When she played the piano, she pressed it against the instrument's soundboard to make out the sound of the notes.

The success of Melville's books and private lessons allowed the family to maintain both a country house and a large apartment in Edinburgh. It was in such comfortable surroundings that their three children were raised: the youngest Edward, the oldest Melville (called Melly), and the middle child, Aleck. He was born in the family's Edinburgh apartment on March 3, 1847—the same year as another famous inventor, Thomas Edison. As Aleck's wife would say much later, "They lived in the very best part of the city, their windows looking over the beautiful gardens… along the top of one of the ridges on which the city is built."[2]

Aleck's curiosity was present early, although not always with positive results. As a toddler, he once wandered into a wheat field, wondering if he could hear it grow. He couldn't. All he could manage to do was get thoroughly lost amidst the stalks that were far taller than he was. Dazed and confused, he wandered sobbing, eventually crying himself to sleep. Finally his father's clear booming voice provided an escape. The memory of wandering aimlessly without any direction haunted Aleck for years.

Aleck probably heard his father's loud voice again when Melville mentioned that his pocket watch needed cleaning. Overhearing his father, Aleck got out a brush, a cake of soap and a bowl of water. He then took the watch apart and gave it a good scrubbing. Needless to say this wasn't what Melville had in mind!

Unfortunately, Aleck's energy and curiosity sometimes exceeded his abilities as he was growing up. He read and learned to play the piano from his mother. He imagined becoming a professional musician—partly because he was talented, partly to shake up his parents. He watched as his father gave speech lessons, and experimented with photography, a new science that was just starting to take off in Edinburgh. Mainly, though, Aleck often seemed as if he was in the way.

He found a partner in mischief with young Ben Herdman, whose father, John, owned a flour mill. In their free time the two boys often played loudly around the mill. Eventually John Herdman had enough. He called the boys into his office and gave them a stern talking to, concluding with the advice that they should find something more useful to do than make a bunch of noise. Always thinking, Aleck wondered what that should be. Well, Herdman said, perhaps they could figure out how to separate the wheat husks from the wheat.

The two youngsters got to work. First they experimented with a small brush. Even though it worked, it was almost as time-consuming as doing it by hand. Then they came upon a giant unused vat with a paddle inside while exploring the flour mill. By attaching brushes to the paddles, dumping in unhusked wheat and working the paddle, they were able to solve Herdman's problem.

"It was a proud day for us when we boys marched into Mr. Herdman's office, presented him with a sample of our cleaned wheat and suggested paddling the wheat," Aleck recalled. "Herdman's injunction to do something useful was my first incentive to invention, and the method of cleaning wheat was the first fruit of my efforts."[3]

The device Aleck and Ben invented would be used at the mill for the next half century.

About the same time, Aleck began attending Edinburgh's Royal High School. Up to that point he had been home-schooled. Unfortunately, the middle child remained in his older brother's shadow. Melly was an academic star, winning numerous awards. Aleck had little but poor grades to show for his time at school by the time he graduated at the age of 14. He hated Classical Greek. He hated Latin. However, he admitted later that studying these "dead languages" prepared him for the terms used in the sciences he loved, like botany and zoology—the study of plants and animals.

Because he didn't do well in school, Aleck probably wanted to set himself apart in some other way. His parents hadn't given him a middle name. So when a family friend named Alexander Graham paid the Bells a visit, Aleck decided to adopt Graham as his middle name.

Melville was displeased with his son's academic achievements. After Aleck left school in 1862, his father sent him to London to live with his grandfather. At the age of 15, Aleck was profoundly influenced by the year he spent in the big city. He arrived dressed like a country boy in battered tweeds. Alexander would have none of that. He quickly bought the boy a stylish jacket and top hat. Aleck was required to wear them and carry a walking cane whenever he went out. Besides dressing Aleck in the best clothes, Alexander educated him in some of the best writers, teaching him Shakespeare and other works he'd once performed as an actor. Slowly, the older gentleman began the training that enabled Aleck to enter the family profession: speech therapy.

"This period of my life seems the turning point of my whole career," Aleck later wrote. "It converted me from a boy somewhat prematurely into a man."[4]

The year did more than that. When his father visited, the three Bell men went to see Sir Charles Wheatstone, a well-known scientist who claimed to have invented a machine that could speak words. Most similar machines were fakes. They enclosed a midget, or a ventriloquist would throw his voice and make it look like the machine was "speaking." Wheatstone didn't do this. His device was the real deal. It was crude but it worked. Aleck could understand the words as they came out. More importantly, he realized a new ambition.

As soon as Aleck returned home, he enlisted his older brother's help in creating their own speaking machine. Using a human skull for a model, he and Melly made their own mouth and voice box from a hard rubber-like

Charles Wheatstone, shown here, was a well-known scientist with a great deal of musical interest. He claimed to invent a machine that could speak words and when Alec visited Wheatstone, he was inspired to create his own "speaking machine."

material and then connected it to a bellows they controlled with a keyboard. The bellows pumped air over the "mouth," sounding just like a crying baby saying "Mama." When anxious neighbors rushed over, worried about the "infant," the mischievous Bell brothers knew they'd succeeded.

Unfortunately, Aleck's father didn't see his son's inventing as anything more than teenage hi-jinks. Inventing wasn't the career he'd mapped out for Aleck, indeed for any of his sons. By 1864, Melville had completed his Visible Speech System and he enlisted his boys as demonstrators.

They'd wait outside lecture halls while their father explained the system and asked audience members to suggest words or sounds. He'd write the symbols for each suggestion on a board and then invite the boys back in. Without hesitation they were able to pronounce everything from foreign words to recreating a yawn. Aleck even successfully pronounced the "Sanskrit Cerebral T," considered one of the toughest sounds for an English speaker to make.

Their demonstrations helped make the system successful, which also helped Melville sell more textbooks and increased his reputation. Not long after Melville died, playwright George Bernard Shaw acknowledged his influence in the preface to the play *Pygmalion*. It is the story of a Cockney woman and an English professor who changes her accent to make her

Aleck mistakenly believed that a device made by Hermann von Helmholtz (pictured here) not only produced vowel sounds, but transmitted them. Because of his mistake, he came to believe in the feasibility of telegraphic transmission of speech.

sound more refined. The play later became a popular movie and musical, *My Fair Lady.*

Back home, Aleck began teaching music and elocution at a school named Weston House. It was on the northern coast of Scotland in the town of Elgin, about 100 miles by road from Edinburgh. He eventually received seventy pounds per year (about 150 dollars, a decent but not princely wage). His grandfather's influence paid off—few of his students suspected their teacher was scarcely older than they were.

Still, Aleck wasn't completely serious. When he wasn't teaching his students to speak, he was teaching the family dog. Over several months he taught it to bark for food, then once it was used to barking "on cue" he began manipulating its mouth. By holding the animal's tongue and jaw in a certain way, its barks could be made to sound like words. Whenever neighbors dropped by, they wanted to hear the dog that asked, "How are you?"

Sadly in 1865, Aleck's grandfather died. Shortly thereafter, the family moved to London so Melville could take over his deceased father's business. Aleck continued his experiments. Looking at how sounds are formed in the mouth, he studied Hermann von Helmholtz who'd done work using tuning forks to determine the musical sounds of instruments.

There was one major problem. Helmholtz's books were written in German. Aleck didn't understand the language. Still he was sure he'd figured out the man's work by looking at the book's detailed illustrations. The language barrier actually helped him out as Aleck stumbled on the kind of lucky accident many inventors have. Studying the drawings, he concluded Helmholtz had transmitted vowels electronically. While this conclusion was mistaken, it gave him a belief that would bear fruit in just over a decade.

"I came to believe firmly in the feasibility of the telegraphic transmission of speech, and I used to tell my friends that someday we should talk by telegraph,"[5] he said.

Even as Aleck progressed in his careers and discoveries, a very real cloud hung over him and his brothers. Both Edinburgh and London suffered from overcrowding and pollution, dangerous side effects of the Industrial Revolution. As farmers became factory workers, they pushed into the cities and packed tightly together in increasing numbers. The factories that employed them spewed smoke and pollution far and wide. Combined with the already moist climate, the conditions were practically a recipe for one of the most contagious and deadly diseases of the nineteenth century: tuberculosis.

The three Bell boys had suffered various illnesses throughout their adolescence, and by the time they were in their late teens their conditions worsened. At the age of eighteen, Edward grew sicker and sicker. Shortly after being diagnosed with tuberculosis, he died.

Three years later in 1870, Melly died from the same disease. He left behind a young widow and a baby. He also left behind the last surviving Bell brother, an inventive dreamer whose health seemed as bad as the health of his two brothers.

Melville and Eliza realized they needed to take drastic action to save him. They wanted to leave the wet and polluted climate behind. They convinced Aleck that he had to come with them, all the way to North America and an uncertain future.

Thomas Edison is one of this country's most famous inventors. Born in 1847, his first job was as a telegraph operator and his first invention was an electric vote recorder. He went on to invent the light bulb, motion picture camera, motion picture projector and many other things. By the time of his death in 1931, he had been issued more than 1,300 individual patents. However, two of his efforts were greatly improved upon by Aleck.

Thomas Edison

Because of his work as a telegraph operator, Edison invented a printer that connected to a telegraph machine. His work with that apparatus inspired him to invent a device capable of receiving and transmitting multiple messages. It was this device that Aleck was trying to craft when he began working on the telephone. By inventing a system that could send four messages at once, Edison beat Aleck in that race.

Of course, Aleck's telephone would make the telegraph all but obsolete. The Western Union Company tried to combine Edison's patent with several others to prove they owned the rights to the telephone. They lost that case, but the paths of the two inventors soon crossed again.

While working on the telegraph, Edison realized if an indented cylinder was spun fast enough it sounded a great deal like someone's voice. Maybe a voice could be recreated. That led to the invention of the phonograph in 1877. Aleck realized that he had come very close to inventing the same thing.

Edison's invention had several problems. The sound quality wasn't very good, the cylinders were fragile, and they quickly wore out. Within a few years, Aleck and his associates invented flat round disks that greatly improved sound quality and durability. They worked so much better than the original that Edison eventually paid Aleck for the right to manufacture them.

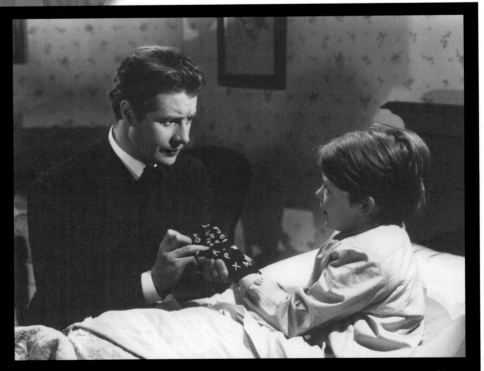

This is a scene from the movie of Alexander Graham Bell's life. In real life, Alec made the finger-spelling glove you see here for his pupil George Sanders. By pointing to the letters on the glove, Alec could communicate with George in public without it being obvious that the boy was deaf.

3

Varied Lessons

Less than a week after their arrival in Canada, Melville Bell paid $2600 for a new home. A great amount in those days, it bought a considerable place—a large house in Brantford, Ontario with a view of a river surrounded by ten wooded acres. Located forty-five miles from Buffalo, New York, the new home did wonders for Aleck's health. Within a few months he had recovered. That made him restless and he looked for something to do. With his father's aid, he soon embarked on a series of teaching assignments across New England. It was more than just a career opportunity. It was a chance for Aleck to demonstrate the Visual Speech System. So even as Aleck worked for various headmasters, he was also working for his father.

The next April, Aleck arrived in the city that would change his life: Boston, Massachusetts. Boston was a center for educational and scientific achievement, ranging from the nation's oldest university—Harvard in nearby Cambridge—to various experiments funded by wealthy citizens. There was probably no better place in the world for Aleck to embark on an inventing career.

Already telegraphy, established more than a quarter of a century earlier, was reaching its limits. The system had been wired across much of the country, and with considerable difficulty had even stretched across the

A Mohawk Indian Village is depicted here. During a hiking trip, Aleck met a group of Mohawk Indians. They made him an honorary member of their tribe. Throughout his life, Aleck would sometimes celebrate his accomplishments by doing a war dance he learned from the Mohawk Indians.

Atlantic Ocean. Yet the expense combined with the difficulty of getting only a single message through a single wire severely limited its future.

There had to be a better way.

At first Aleck wasn't thinking much about inventing. His thoughts were on teaching. At this he excelled. Somewhat shy and nervous around strangers, before a classroom he shone. He could be playful and fun, while making sure his students learned. He was still interested in his own learning. During a hiking trip, he met a group of Mohawk Indians. They were pleased that the young man was interested in their language. In return, they made him an honorary member of the tribe and taught him their war dance. In future years, he would sometimes astonish acquaintances by breaking into the dance when he did something he was especially proud of.

In the spring of 1872, he taught briefly at the Clarke School for the Deaf in Northampton, about 50 miles west of Boston, and impressed the school's president, a lawyer named Gardiner Greene Hubbard. By that fall he was back in Boston and opened up a school to work with private clients. George Sanders was among the first ones he took on. He also wrote articles on educating deaf people based on his own experiences.

By 1873, Aleck felt torn. Every step of young George's Sanders' progress excited him. Often he wrote his parents about the work he was doing, believing that the techniques he was using with George would eventually help many other deaf students. He experimented with combining learning and play, and constructed a glove with all the letters of the alphabet. George could spell a word just by pointing to various places on his teacher's hand.

Yet even as he taught George, Aleck's mind began to spin with ideas. He'd never forgotten the thrill of creating something new, something "useful." He imagined a device combining current technology like that used in telegraphy with improvements based on what he'd learned as a pianist and as an educator.

So the telephone began, like many inventions, with the simple idea of enhancing an existing product. In this case, Aleck wondered about sending multiple messages over the same telegraph wire.

Beginning with "What hath God wrought?"—Samuel Morse's famous message on May 24, 1844 that began telegraph service—creative men had dreamed of improving that invention. As telegraph wires began criss-crossing North America, inventors knew there was a better way. They just had to discover it.

For years, inventors such as Thomas Edison and Joseph Stearns wrestled with creating a multiple telegraph that could send more than a single message at a time. Edison had a falling out with his Boston partners and left the city in 1869. That left Stearns, whose "duplex telegraph"

sent two signals at once and was promptly bought by telegraph giant Western Union.

Aleck knew he could do more than send just a pair of signals across a line. He purchased the necessary equipment and began a series of experiments. He hoped the invention would give him his freedom. He was in his twenties, quite ready to be completely on his own and not at his father's command. Unfortunately, when Alexander wrote his father about his multiple telegraph experiments, Melville Bell told his son not to waste his time.

By January of the next year, Aleck learned of Martin Loomis, who'd devised a system that could send a message from the ground to an airborne kite. While wildly impractical, it looked to Aleck like a step in the right direction.

Even as Loomis lost much of his financial backing, Aleck was on his way to getting money of his own. Throughout 1873, he divided his time among teaching private students like George Sanders, working as an elocution professor at Boston University, and reading everything he could about electricity and sound waves. J. Baile's popular book on electricity made him recall the piano lessons he'd taken from his mother. "I was familiar with the fact that when we sing a vowel sign into a piano, while the pedal is depressed, the piano reproduces not only the pitch, but approximately the quality of the vowel uttered,"[1] he said.

Aleck also recalled his boyhood, when he'd pressed his lips against his deaf mother's forehead and spoken to her. She'd been able to understand him because her bones conducted the vibrations of his words. Surely there was a way to do the same thing with electrical wires.

"Leave the beaten track occasionally, and dive into the woods," Aleck later advised. "Every time you do so you will be certain to find something that you have never seen before."[2]

Aleck wasn't sure if he wanted to just build a multiple telegraph device. He considered constructing a machine to reproduce human speech. He'd experimented with a xylophone-like device that vibrated when someone spoke and conducted the sounds along an electrical current. It

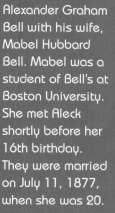

Alexander Graham Bell with his wife, Mabel Hubbard Bell. Mabel was a student of Bell's at Boston University. She met Aleck shortly before her 16th birthday. They were married on July 11, 1877, when she was 20.

was far from what he'd eventually invent, but already he was further along than his competitors. Although he was as poorly educated about electricity as Morse had been, Aleck at least understood the way the energy could conduct sound.

Unfortunately, everything ground to a halt when he tried to file a patent caveat with the United States Patent Office. Obtaining a patent would mean that no one else could sell or manufacture Aleck's invention without his permission. A patent caveat just announced that he was on his way to inventing something—in this case, a multiple telegraph. Unfortunately, he wasn't allowed to file such a form because he wasn't born in the United States. He could only file a patent. But in order to do that, he had to actually invent something.

It was disappointing enough that for a while he abandoned his work on the multiple telegraph, and focused on the speech device—the device that would someday become a telephone.

Everyone around him noticed the young man's drive. His energy was of particular interest to a young woman named Mabel Hubbard. She was the daughter of Gardiner Greene Hubbard, the Clarke School headmaster he'd impressed in 1872. She'd become deaf after a childhood bout with scarlet fever. Now she was one of Aleck's students. The sixteen-year-old noted in a letter, "He has his machine running beautifully but it will kill him if he isn't careful."[3]

Although Aleck's machine wasn't really running "beautifully," it soon would be. And Mabel Hubbard would have a lot to do with it.

Scarlet fever begins mostly with a rash. Bright red, or scarlet—which is where the name came from—that rash spreads across the sick person's body. Then, like skin flaking away after a case of sunburn, it disappears.

Unfortunately, in the 1800s this wasn't the end of scarlet fever. The flaking was only the beginning. The scarlet part might have been over. But the fever continued, growing until it reached temperatures in excess of 101 degrees. Highly contagious, it often infected entire families, killing half or even more of them. During the second half of the nineteenth century it was the leading cause of death among children aged two or over.

In fact, Aleck himself caught it as a child, and even remembered seeing what he was sure was a ghost standing by his bedside. Such hallucinations are common with people suffering from high fevers. He recovered without suffering any lasting ill effects. But many other people, including Mabel Hubbard, weren't so lucky. She suffered deafness, a result of the disease.

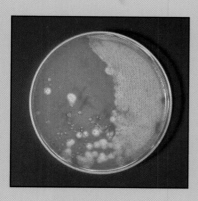

In the 1920s, George Frederick Dick and Gladys Henry Dick, an American husband and wife team of physicians, isolated the specific bacteria that caused scarlet fever. In 1923 they were able to develop a method of immunization to treat it. In the following year, they developed a procedure known as the Dick Test to determine susceptibility or immunity to scarlet fever by an injection of scarlet fever toxin. George and Gladys were nominated for the Nobel Prize in Medicine in 1925 for their research.

Today penicillin or other types of antibiotics are used to successfully treat the illness. It is hardly ever fatal.

Elisha Gray, depicted here in this drawing, was one of many inventors to lay claim to inventing the telephone. Mr. Gray filed his papers at the patent office after Bell, and at one point, wrote to Bell, telling him, "I do not... claim even the credit of inventing it," but later joined Western Union in a lawsuit challenging Bell's claim to the telephone.

4

Phoning Watson

It was the summer of 1874, and Alexander Graham Bell was playing with a dead man's ear. He had taken it from a body given to him by Clarence Blake, a Boston ear specialist. He attached one end of a piece of straw to the bones in the inner ear and the other end to a phonautograph, a machine that traced lines on a piece of paper, responding to the sound waves that came through the ear.

Aleck had moved a step closer. If straw could conduct sound waves, then an undulating current of electricity should do even better. This type of current, which moves in an up-and-down motion, would be similar to a sound wave. So wires might be able to carry the human voice.

Aleck had gotten as far as he could on his own. Now he needed partners. Fortunately the young inventor didn't have to look far. He first went to George's father, Thomas Sanders. Sanders agreed to provide funding. Then he approached Mabel Hubbard's father. His specialty was patent law. Aleck had gone just seeking legal advice, but he soon came out of the meeting with another partner.

There was just one problem. Neither man wanted Aleck to focus on his "speaking machine." They wanted him to concentrate on a multiple tele-graph.

Quietly, Hubbard checked to see if there were any patents out on multiple telegraph machines and learned that Elisha Gray had filed a patent caveat. Not only was he working on a device similar to Aleck, he had the financial backing of both Western Union *and* Western Electric.

"He has the advantage over me in being a practical electrician," Aleck noted modestly, "but I have reason to believe I am better acquainted with the phenomenon of sound than he is—so I have an advantage there."[1]

Although Aleck still insisted he could eventually "telegraph" the human voice, Hubbard and Sanders insisted that he focus on the simpler (and seemingly more profitable) multiple telegraph. His father just wanted him to stop messing around with crazy inventions and get back to teaching his Visual Speech System.

"Your wisest course would be to sell your plans to Messrs. Sanders and Hubbard...You can't work out the scheme without neglecting your other business. Take what you can get at once!"[2] his father ordered.

Aleck was soon able to ignore all of the advice, all of the demands. Gray beat him to the patent with the multiple telegraph. But during a trip to Washington, D.C. Aleck had a meeting with Joseph Henry, a well-known electrical scientist. Henry listened to Aleck's ideas for a voice telegraph and encouraged him to pursue his invention, not letting his ignorance about electricity hold him back. Back in Boston, Aleck began working every free minute, laboring to create a device to transmit the voice.

By now he had practical help. Thomas Watson had become Aleck's assistant in January of 1875. An electrician who was good with his hands, Watson had the technical know-how to turn his boss's dreams into reality. The two met a few months earlier when Aleck went to have a model designed at the shop where Watson worked. The young inventor made an immediate impression.

"He was a tall, slender, quick motioned young man," Watson later said, "with a pale face, black side whiskers and drooping moustache, big nose and high sloping forehead crowned with bushy jet black hair."[3]

Six months later, on June 2, 1875, Aleck and Watson were working in their laboratory with reeds, which are thin metal strips that produce a single note when plucked. The reeds were connected to multiple telegraph transmitters and electrical currents. At this moment, though, the current was turned off and Watson plucked a reed while Aleck carefully listened in the other room.

Aleck's musical training came in handy. He recognized the sound of the particular reed and realized that a complex sound—such as a person's voice—could actually create its own current and travel through the wire before becoming a sound again at the opposite end.

Aleck quickly sketched a device he called a "gallows telephone." It wouldn't carry a conversation, but it *would* carry sounds. This was a step in the right direction. Although he'd drawn a sketch of the instrument, he took forever to build it. Hubbard fretted that if they didn't file a patent soon someone would beat them to it.

He was almost right.

On February 14, 1876, Hubbard filed an unfinished patent application—it had just enough information to qualify. Less than two hours later, Elsiha Gray tried to file a similar patent for a device he called the "speaking telegraph." However, his ideas weren't developed enough to become a working telephone. Aleck's ideas were.

"Improvements in Telegraphy" was the first patent filed for a telephone. It was granted on March 7, 1876, and for the next nineteen years Aleck and his partners—Hubbard, Sanders, and now Watson—would share in any profits from its sale or manufacture.

Three days later, Aleck stood next to a slightly modified design. He told Watson to go into another room and listen at a duplicate of his machine. Aleck leaned into his "phone," and said "Mr. Watson, come here. I want to see you."

Moments later, a jubilant Watson came in from the other room. Aleck knew it worked. Now he just had to convince people to buy it.

June 25, 1876 was a very notable date in U.S. history. On a hillside above the Little Bighorn River in Montana, U.S. Army Colonel George Armstrong Custer and more than 200 of his cavalrymen were annihilated in what become known as Custer's Last Stand. At about the same time in Philadelphia, more than 2,000 miles to the east, the Centennial Exhibition opened. It was the beginning of a long celebration honoring the signing of the Declaration of Independence one hundred years earlier. It was the perfect place to show off the telephone. Unfortunately, Aleck didn't submit his application in time. He couldn't get a spot in the electrical section. He had to settle for a booth at the educational wing, down a long hot hallway from all the other inventors and scientists. It took some work to convince the judges and other dignitaries to check out Aleck's new invention.

Once they heard it with their own ears, they could barely believe it. "My God, it talks," exclaimed the surprised Brazilian emperor, Dom Pedro.

Less than four months later, Aleck and Watson took part in the first "long-distance" call. It was between Boston and Cambridge, a distance of about three miles.

After some initial hesitation, Aleck's invention began to take off. Factories lined up to build it. Telephone lines were strung alongside the telegraph lines they'd soon replace.

For his part, Aleck celebrated by marrying his student, Mabel Hubbard. Their love had taken some time to develop. Her father was a bit worried about Aleck, who was nearly thirty, marrying his teenage daughter. Mr. Hubbard finally gave his blessing and they were married in his living room on July 11, 1877. Aleck gained a wife and lost a letter. At Mabel's request, he dropped the final "k" in his name so the spelling would seem more "American."

Honeymooning in England, the couple was received by Queen Victoria. She was impressed with Alec's demonstration of his new invention and asked that telephones be installed in her palace. Alec was pleased with his success. By then, of course, he was already imagining other inventions.

FYInfo

Alexander Graham Bell was granted the first patent for the telephone. But he may not have invented it. Many people believe that that honor belongs to Antonio Meucci.

Born in Florence, Italy in 1808, Meucci became a theater stage technician and came to Havana, Cuba in 1835. By accident, he discovered that electricity could be used as a voice conductor. Developing his "speaking telegraph" would become an obsession, especially after he moved to the United States in 1850. He spent every spare dollar and every spare minute honing it. He even connected a phone line from his workshop to his sick wife's bedroom in 1855.

Antonio Meucci

The problem was money. Despite numerous efforts, he couldn't get anyone to help him produce and market his invention. Then he was involved in an accident that left him severely burned. While he lay helpless, his wife sold his telephones for six dollars.

He refused to admit defeat. In 1871, he filed a patent caveat. By then he had become a citizen and was entitled to, whereas Aleck was not. But the patent caveat had to be renewed every year. In 1874 he couldn't afford the ten-dollar fee. Two years later, Aleck unveiled his device and Western Union signed a deal with him. Western Union already had Meucci's plans and he sued. The case made it to the United States Supreme Court, but died when Meucci did in 1889.

Meucci's telephone, said to have been made in the year 1857, as reported in *Scientific American*, 1884.

On September 25, 2001 the United States House of Representatives passed a resolution honoring him for his "work in the invention of the telephone," noting that, "Where as if Meucci had been able to pay the $10 fee to maintain the caveat after 1874, no patent could have been issued to Bell."[4]

This famous photograph shows Alec making the first long-distance call from New York to Chicago in 1892, opening a permanent long-distance network.

5

Always the Inventor

Mabel and Alexander Graham Bell stayed in Europe for over a year. Alec demonstrated the telephone to packed lecture halls across the continent. He also showed off his father's Visual Speech System—no matter how successful Alec became, he always felt obligated to his father.

Alec seemed to pause only for his wife to give birth—their first child was born on May 10, 1878. They named her Elsie May. The couple would have another daughter, Marian Daisy, who was born two years later.

Six months after Elsie's birth, the couple returned to the United States. They arrived to chaos. An anxious Tom Watson greeted the Bells at the docks. There was trouble.

Despite the patent, Western Union was selling their own version of the telephone. They claimed a combination of inventors, including Thomas Edison and Elisha Gray. In order to prove he'd invented it, Alec had to go to court. Going to court would soon become a familiar routine for the inventor. All told, he appeared in some 600 legal actions. In one case alone, his testimony ran to over 400 pages. In all of them, the Bell Telephone Company prevailed. In the Western Union case, a letter from Gray admitting that Bell was the sole inventor of the telephone helped him. Once again Alec had the opportunity to do his Mohawk war dance.

Considering how often he had to defend his patent, it's surprising Alec had time for anything else. But he did. Because of the success of the Bell Telephone Company (which eventually became the American Telephone and Telegraph Company, or AT&T), Alec became a millionaire. He never had to work again. Of course, Alec didn't consider what he did as "work."

He was still interested in helping deaf people. In 1879 he invented the audiometer, a device used to measure hearing levels. His name became incorporated into the word "decibel," which refers to units of sound measurement.

His next major invention came from tragedy. President James Garfield had been shot in the back by an assassin in July 1881. Although the bullet hadn't killed him, it remained lodged somewhere near his spine and the president was in critical condition. In that era, there were no X-rays to determine the bullet's exact location, no clean surgical probes. There were only the unwashed hands of the doctors, poking around the wound as they tried to find the bullet. One of them wondered if Alec could invent something better.

Using some of the same technology from the telephone, Alec invented the world's first metal detector. After several successful lab tests, he used it on the president. But this time it didn't work. All he heard was a steady hum. Garfield finally died on September 19. Soon afterward, Alec discovered the problem. Coil spring mattresses had just been introduced, and the metal was the reason for the steady hum. Many people believe that if the president had been placed on a table or the floor—where there was no metal—Alec's device would have quickly located the bullet. Although it didn't save the president's life, his metal detector would soon be widely used in hospitals and help to save the lives of thousands of other people.

Alec's next invention also came from tragedy. This time the tragedy was closer to home. His son Edward was born prematurely a few weeks after Garfield had been shot. The tiny infant could barely breathe and died within a few hours. Alec invented a device he called the "vacuum jacket" so that other parents wouldn't have to endure the sadness he and Mabel felt. With improvements, it eventually became the iron lung, a device that kept many polio victims alive before Dr. Jonas Salk invented the polio vaccine in the 1950s.

Alec's interests went beyond medicine and communication. He helped found *Science* Magazine, and assisted Mabel's father in founding the National Geographic Society. After Hubbard died, Alec took over the presidency of the Society and was instrumental in transforming its magazine from a rather boring, scholarly publication to the more dynamic and exciting magazine familiar to readers today.

Alec and Mabel settled in Baddeck, Nova Scotia in 1886 and began buying up land. Eventually they developed an estate they named Beinn Bhreagh (pronounced Ben Vreeah), which is Gaelic for "beautiful mountains." Once there, Alec began working toward the dream he'd had on his honeymoon when he'd imagined great flying machines. He experimented with carefully designed kites using the kinds of architecture that would someday support bridges. These kites were built with human flight in mind. But when the Wright brothers flew the first aircraft in 1903 at Kitty Hawk, North Carolina, Alec realized that kite travel was far too slow to be practical.

"Circumstances arise that bend our lives hither or thither against our will," Alec would later tell his son-in-law Gilbert. "But our lives are bent, not broken—there is always continuity of growth. In looking back over my own life I realize how different has been the result from anything that I aimed at, and yet I can recognize continuity in the whole; one occupation has fitted me for the next, and that again for the next."[1]

He would find a way to keep inventing, no matter what the circumstances. Now he put his energy into improving the airplane. With several partners he constructed aircraft that broke records. One of them was known as the Silver Dart. The first plane to fly in Canada, it traveled half a mile during its maiden flight in 1909 and reached a speed of forty miles per hour.

Not content to set records in the air, Alec turned to water. Along with partner Casey Baldwin, he developed a hydrofoil, a kind of boat that uses ski-like foils to lift the hull above the water when it reaches a certain speed. During a test in 1919, it reached a speed of seventy-one miles per hour, the fastest a boat had ever gone!

Besides inventing, he continued to teach and lecture. He championed the education system of Maria Montessori. It was a style very similar to his own, as it emphasized learning through discovery and play. In 1912, Alec was instrumental in opening the first Montessori school in Canada.

Two years later, Alec was the first person to use the phrase "greenhouse effect." This term, which describes the way the planet could possibly trap heat beneath a haze of pollution, opposed many popular views of the time. Scientists in the early 1900s believed that the pollution created by fossil fuels like oil and coal would wrap around the earth and keep it cool. Alec believed the opposite. He thought that just as a greenhouse trapped heat, the planet would do the same. Today, many scientists view the greenhouse effect as fact. He was also among the first prominent people to demonstrate the importance of conserving and recycling energy.

He had one final role to play in the history of the telephone. In 1915, he and Watson had another phone conversation, similar to their first one thirty-nine years earlier. Alec was in New York, while his former assistant was in San Francisco. They were participating in the formal ceremonies that marked the completion of the first coast-to-coast telephone line.

During the conversation, Alec repeated his famous first words: "Mr. Watson, come here. I want to see you." Watson replied humorously that it would take him nearly a week rather than a minute because they were so far apart.

Few people realized how much Aleck was suffering by this time. He had diabetes, and the only treatment for it in the early 1900s was a very low-calorie diet. Overweight for much of his life, Aleck had a hard time sticking to the diet. Slowly his organs began to fail.

On August 2, 1922, Aleck died from complications of diabetes. He was buried two days later. At precisely 6:25 p.m., in the midst of the funeral services, all the phones in the United States were silenced for one minute in his honor.

Jane Goodall

Founded on January 13, 1888 by thirty-three men at the Cosmos Club not far from the White House in Washington, D.C., the National Geographic Society was designed to increase and diffuse geographical knowledge.

Its founders included, in the Society's own words in its website, "The first explorers of the Grand Canyon and Yellowstone, those who had carried the American Flag farthest north, who had measured the altitude of our famous mountains, traced the windings of our coasts and rivers, determined the distribution of flora and fauna and enlightened us in the customs of the aborigines and marked out the path of storm and flood."[2]

Yet the first president was not an adventurer or an explorer. He was a lawyer, Gardiner Green Hubbard, Alec's father-in-law.

Nine months later, the first National Geographic magazine was published. It was a very technical scientific journal that appealed mainly to scientists. When Alec became president of the Society in 1898, he wanted to use the magazine to convey his personal excitement about geography. He hired a young man named Gilbert Grosvenor, who later became his son-in-law. During Grosvenor's 55 years as editor, it became the popular, full-color magazine that millions of people read today and which is world-famous for the high quality of its photography. The Society also publishes World, Traveler, Adventure and National Geographic for Kids.

Robert Ballard

Through the years, the Society has sponsored many scientific expeditions, such as the first airplane flight over the South Pole, Jane Goodall's many years living with chimpanzees in Africa and Robert Ballard's discovery of the sunken luxury liner Titanic. It is the world's largest non-profit educational and scientific organization.

Chronology

1847 Born in Edinburgh, Scotland on March 3

1857 Begins attending Edinburgh's Royal High School

1858 Takes the middle name Graham after one of his father's friends whom he admires

1862 Is sent to live with his grandfather, Alexander

1864 Builds a speaking machine along with brother Melly

1867 Brother Edward dies

1870 Brother Melville dies; the family leaves Scotland for Brantford, Ontario

1871 Starts teaching career in the United States

1874 Begins work with phonautograph and harmonic telegraph

1875 Transmits sound through harmonic telegraph

1876 Granted a patent for "Improvements in Telegraphy;" has his first telephone conversation with Watson and gives the first public demonstration of the telephone at Philadelphia's Centennial Exposition

1877 Marries Mabel Hubbard; forms Bell Telephone Company

1878 Daughter Elsie May is born

1879 Moves to Washington, D.C.

1880 Daughter Marian (Daisy) is born; receives the Volta Prize

1881 Invents telephonic probe and vacuum jacket

1882 Becomes U.S. citizen

1891 Begins flight experiments near new Nova Scotia home

1898 Becomes president of the National Geographic Society

1909 Silver Dart airplane becomes first airplane to fly in Canada

1910 Begins hydrofoil experiments

1919 HD-4 hydrofoil sets world water speed record of 70.86 miles per hour

1922 Dies from complications of diabetes on August 2

Timeline of Discovery

1752 Benjamin Franklin designs the lightning rod to use in his experiments with electricity.

1753 An anonymous letter in Scots Magazine proposes transmitting words by ringing bells at the end of an electrically charged wire.

1790s The U.S. government offers a prize to the designer of an Atlantic Coast communications system, calling it the telegraph.

1831 Joseph Henry publishes an article detailing how he rang a bell by opening and closing an electrical circuit.

1844 Telegraph designer Samuel Morse transmits his first message: "What hath God wrought?"

1854 Charles Bourseul suggests the development of an electric telephone.

1861 Philip Reis invents a device he calls "Telephon" that can transmit electrical tones through wires.

1866 Using light gauge copper wire, West Virginia dentist Mahlon Loomis transmits a message from one kite to another 18 miles away.

1876 Alexander Graham Bell invents the telephone.

1877 The Bell Telephone Company is formed.

1885 The American Telegraph and Telephone Company is formed as part of Bell.

1894 Alexander Graham Bell's second telephone patent expires, clearing the way for competition. Within ten years there will be 6,000 companies across the United States.

1915 The first transcontinental phone line is opened.

1919 The first dial telephones are installed.

1934 Telephone service between the U.S. and Japan begins.

1947 The concept for cellular telephones is first developed.

1948 AT&T offers networking services for television.

1958 The first commercial modem is introduced.

1963 Touchtone phone service begins.

1965 Early Bird, the first commercial communications satellite, goes into orbit.

1968 The 911 emergency dialing system is inaugurated.

1983 The first commercial cellular telephone system begins.

1995 The number of cellular subscribers in the United States exceeds twenty-five million.

2000 Data traffic exceeds voice traffic for the first time.

2003 Nationwide optical networks are installed.

Chapter Notes

Chapter One: An Important Lesson

1. Edwin Grosvenor and Morgan Wesson, *Alexander Graham Bell: The Life and Times of the Man Who Invented the Telephone*, (New York: Harry N. Abrams, 1977), p. 40.

2. Ibid., p. 41.

3. James Mackay, *Alexander Graham Bell: A Life*, (New York: John Wiley and Sons, Inc., 1997), p. 34.

Chapter Two: Parts of Speech

1. Tom L. Matthews, *Always Inventing: A Photobiography of Alexander Graham Bell*, (Washington, D.C.: National Geographic Society, 1999), p. 10.

2. Edwin Grosvenor and Morgan Wesson, *Alexander Graham Bell: The Life and Times of the Man Who Invented the Telephone*, (New York: Harry N. Abrams, 1977), p. 16.

3. Ibid., p. 17.

4. Ibid., p. 22.

5. Ibid., p. 30.

Chapter Three: Varied Lessons

1. Edwin Grosvenor and Morgan Wesson, *Alexander Graham Bell: The Life and Times of the Man Who Invented the Telephone*, (New York: Harry N. Abrams, 1977), p. 44.

2. http://www.fitzgeraldstudio.com/html/bell/inventor.html

3. Grosvenor and Wesson, p. 44.

4. Naomi Pasachoff, *Alexander Graham Bell: Making Connections*, (New York: Oxford University Press, 1996), p. 65.

Chapter Four: Phoning Watson

1. Edwin Grosvenor and Morgan Wesson, *Alexander Graham Bell: The Life and Times of the Man Who Invented the Telephone*, (New York: Harry N. Abrams, 1977), p. 49.

2. James Mackay, *Alexander Graham Bell: A Life*, (New York: John Wiley and Sons, Inc., 1997), p. 96.

3. Ibid, p. 99.

4. http://www.popular-science.net/history/meucci_congress_resolution.html

Chapter Five: Always the Inventor

1. James Mackay, *Alexander Graham Bell: A Life*, (New York: John Wiley and Sons, Inc., 1997), p. 302.

2. http://www.nationalgeographic.com/siteindex/

Glossary

brogue
strongly accented English, usually associated with Irish and Scots

Cockney
English dialect spoken in parts of London; its most famous characteristic is dropping the letter H at the beginning of a word. For example, the professor in Pygmalion (and later My Fair Lady) is named Henry Higgins. Eliza Doolittle, the play's heroine, calls him Enry Iggins.

current
flow of electrical charge

elocution
(ell-oh-CUE-shun) - art of public speaking

patent
government grant giving an inventor the sole rights to his or her invention

semaphore
(SEM-uh-for) - system of signaling which uses flags

tutorials
(too-TORE-ee-uhls) – lessons given to individuals or small groups

undulate
(UHN-joo-late) - to rise and fall in a smooth, wavelike pattern

46

For Further Reading

For Young Adults:

Durrett, Deanne. *Alexander Graham Bell*. San Diego, CA: KidHaven Press, 2002.

MacLeod, Elizabeth. *Alexander Graham Bell: An Inventive Life*. Tonawanda, NY: Kids Can Press, 1999.

Matthews, Tom L. *Always Inventing: A Photobiography of Alexander Graham Bell*. Washington, D.C.: National Geographic Society, 1999.

Pasachoff, Naomi. *Alexander Graham Bell: Making Connections*. New York: Oxford University Press, 1996.

Works Consulted:

Bruce, Robert V. *Alexander Graham Bell and The Conquest of Solitude*. Ithaca, New York: Cornell University Press, 1993.

Eber, Dorothy. *Genius at Work, Images of Alexander Graham Bell*. New York: Viking Press, 1982.

Grosvenor, Edwin and Morgan Wesson. *Alexander Graham Bell: The Life and Times of the Man Who Invented the Telephone*. New York: Harry N. Abrams, 1997.

Mackay, James. *Alexander Graham Bell: A Life*. New York: John Wiley and Sons, Inc., 1997.

On the Internet:

Antonio Meucci
http://www.italianhistorical.org/MeucciStory.htm

Cyber Telephone Museum
http://www.museumphones.com/

Inventing the Telephone
http://www.att.com/history/inventing.html

The Invention of the Telegraph
http://www.memory.loc.gov/ammem/sfbmhtml/sfbmtelessay.html

The Inventor
http://www.fitzgeraldstudio.com/html/bell/inventor.html

National Geographic Society
http://www.nationalgeographic.com/siteindex/

The Telephone: Timeline
http://www.pbs.org/wgbh/amex/technology/techtimeline/

US Congress Resolution on Antonio Meucci
http://www.popular-science.net/history/meucci_congress_resolution.html

Index

MAY – 2 2005

$19⁹⁵